D0483310

In
1935 if you wanted to
read a good book, you needed
either a lot of money or a library card.
Cheap paperbacks were available, but their
poor production generally mirrored the quality
between the covers. One weekend that year,
Allen Lane, Managing Director of The Bodley Head,
having spent the weekend visiting Agatha Christie,
found himself on a platform at Exeter station trying to
find something to read for his journey back to London.
He was appalled by the quality of the material he had to
choose from. Everything that Allen Lane achieved from that
day until his death in 1970 was based on a passionate belief
in the existence of 'a vast reading public for *intelligent*
books at a low price'. The result of his momentous vision
was the birth not only of Penguin, but of the 'paperback
revolution'. Quality writing became available for the price of
a packet of cigarettes, literature became a mass medium
for the first time, a nation of book-borrowers became a
nation of book-buyers – and the very concept of book
publishing was changed for ever. Those founding
principles – of quality and value, with an overarching
belief in the fundamental importance of reading –
have guided everything the company has
done since 1935. Sir Allen Lane's
pioneering spirit is still very much alive
at Penguin in 2005. Here's to
the next 70 years!

MORE THAN A BUSINESS

'We decided it was time to end the almost customary half-hearted manner in which cheap editions were produced – as though the only people who could possibly want cheap editions must belong to a lower order of intelligence. We, however, believed in the existence in this country of a vast reading public for intelligent books at a low price, and staked everything on it'
Sir Allen Lane, 1902–1970

'The Penguin Books are splendid value for sixpence, so splendid that if other publishers had any sense they would combine against them and suppress them'
George Orwell

'More than a business … a national cultural asset'
Guardian

'When you look at the whole Penguin achievement you know that it constitutes, in action, one of the more democratic successes of our recent social history'
Richard Hoggart

Contents

Introduction

Something for the Weekend is my little contribution to celebrate Penguin's seventy years in publishing. My mum said that I probably shouldn't call it this because of the associations with condoms and everything. We certainly couldn't have used a title like this seventy years ago, but times have changed!

Anyway, it's called this because the weekend is when I get an opportunity to cook at home and have a wicked time with my family and friends. And now I've got kids the weekends are so important for cooking with them – I find it really grounding and always have such a laugh with them. Remember – cooking is supposed to be fun and not a chore. So here is a collection of some of my favourite recipes from the books I've written over the past few years. I'm sure you'll have lots of fun with them, so roll your sleeves up and get stuck in.

This collection of recipes couldn't be more apt – it really is 'something for the weekend', whether you're looking for breakfast ideas, snacks, lazy lunches, proper dinner parties or whether you're after a really good party cake recipe.

Have a great weekend cooking.

And Happy Birthday, Penguin.

Love
Jamie O x

Brekkie

Midnight pan-cooked breakfast

Me and this dish go back a long way. To the pre-shaving days of being an under-age drinker down the Wagon and Horses in Saffron Walden with a fake ID and all my village mates. Only once in a while of course. But seriously, without trying to sound like a lagered-up geezer, I think everyone's experienced the need for food around midnight, whether the binge was small or large, otherwise why would kebab shops be so popular in Britain? Anyway, I always used to have three or four friends back to my house for munchies or to stay the night and this dish was devised so we didn't have too much trouble making it or too much washing up to do. In actual fact, I only had to wipe the non-stick pan clean. It also makes its way from the pan to the plate quite quickly, as patience isn't a virtue at that time of night with my mates!

First of all get the biggest non-stick pan available, and preheat it on a high heat while you gather your ingredients. Obviously you wouldn't be organized at this point so it's a matter of using what you've got, but ideally I like to have mushrooms, bacon, tomatoes, sausages and eggs. By the time you have got these together the pan will be hot, so slice your sausages in half lengthways and pat them out flat so they cook quickly. Place into the pan at one side. On the other side, put a tiny lug of oil and place a pile of mushrooms over it which you can rip up or leave whole. Shake the pan about a bit to coat the mushrooms and season with some salt and pepper. Push to one side and then lay some slices of bacon and halved tomatoes in the pan. Cook for a couple more minutes until the bacon is crisp and golden. Shake the pan and turn the bacon over. Now is the time to put a round of toast in the toaster.

At this stage you should respect the rustic and authentic look and shuffle everything about so that it's all mixed together and add 2 or 3 eggs at different ends of the pan. The whites of the eggs will dribble in and around the sausages, bacon, tomatoes and mushrooms. Turn the heat down a little and continue to cook for another minute before placing the pan under the grill and finishing the eggs to your liking. Using a non-stick pan I've always found the removal of this dish to the plate extremely easy – it will resemble a frisbee and will slide on to your plate with no trouble at all. Doesn't that sound appetizing? But honestly, it really is a gem.

Pukkolla

Pukkolla is my name for this outrageously scrumptious concoction. It's one of the best things you can have for breakfast as it's got everything you need to kickstart your day. Basically it's a bastardized, personally composed muesli. The great thing about it is that you can adjust it to your own preference. It's very handy to have a large plastic airtight container to store your composed pukkolla in, so try and get hold of one.

COMPOSING AND PRESERVING

Serves many mornings

8 large handfuls of organic Scottish porridge oats •
2 large handfuls of ground bran • 1 handful of
chopped dried apricots • 1 handful of chopped dried
dates • 1 handful of crumbled walnuts • 1 handful
of smashed or chopped almonds, hazelnuts or
Brazil nuts

Add your porridge oats and bran to your plastic container with the apricots and dates. Add the walnuts and your other chosen nuts (I usually bash them up in a tea towel). At this point feel free to improvise, adding any other preferred dried fruits like raisins, sultanas or figs – but personally I think my combination works pretty well. This will keep for a good couple of months very happily in your airtight container, but you'll have eaten it by then, I guarantee.

MAKING AND KNOCKING TOGETHER

milk to cover • ½ crunchy apple per person,
washed and unpeeled

I would definitely try to make this the night or day before you want to eat it, although it can be made at the time (but you won't get the smooth silky scrumptious texture that the milk gives it overnight). I normally place double the amount of composed cereal I need (i.e. 4 portions for 2 people) into a bowl. Doubling up like this gives you enough to eat for the next couple of days. Cover with milk, grate in around half an apple per person and stir immediately to stop the apple discolouring. Place in the fridge.

Bacon sarnie my stylie

Simple, you may think, but a good bacon sarnie has challenged many chefs, hotels and greasy spoons around the country for years and years. There is a key to this recipe and in my view this is the way to do it.

You need the best dry-cured bacon you can get hold of. This generally means you won't get the shrinkage and watery residue from cooking like you do with most bacon these days. Shame, as we British folk used to be extremely good at rearing and curing good bacon. Second, I would suggest that you try to get hold of thicker-cut bacon; not the wafer-thin stuff that became fashionable a few years ago – you need something you can really get your teeth into. Third, I buy a small, fresh sandwich loaf (gotta be white unless you need your roughage), which should be around 25cm/10 inches long. I then cunningly and politely ask the baker to slice it lengthways, instead of across as normal. I do this all the time and it's great. It's purely a visual thing but it seems to make it taste better to me – I don't know why. I've always been a strange boy.

So, you've got your bacon and your bread. You could quite easily go ahead and cook your bacon and toast your bread under the grill. Lovely. But if you fancy yourself as a bit of a tiger then acquire a ridged griddle pan, which I get as hot as possible (about 4 minutes on the highest heat) and then begin to grill about 4 slices of bacon (per person if you're greedy like me). After about 1 minute you can turn the bacon over and it will be golden with those funky charred marks across which I also think benefit the flavour slightly. Cook the other side for 1 more minute. At this point I shuffle all the bacon up one end of the pan to carry on cooking a little longer while I toast off my 2 long pieces of bread in the pan. What I love about this way of doing it is that the bread soaks up just a little (not a lot) of the fat that has cooked out of the bacon which makes it even more tasty. When it has toasted on both sides you could butter your toast – I don't bother – and lay your bacon across each slice. Squeeze the 2 bits of bread together. Now it's ready to be eaten, preferably with some HP sauce. In the past I have also added halved tomatoes and mushrooms to the pan, which do go down very well in the sarnie too.

Sticky sausage bap with melted cheese and brown sauce

I used to have one of these every morning at 7 a.m. on the way to college at Westminster. Just get 3 half-decent snags (that's sausages to us southerners) and grill them until sticky and crispy on all sides. Remove to a plate, cut them in half, and line them up in the grill tray in the shape of your bap. Cover evenly with a good handful of grated mild Cheddar cheese and put back under the grill for the cheese to melt. Slice your bap in half, butter both sides, and smear outrageously with brown sauce. Using a knife, place your sausages and melted cheese on the brown sauce side of the bap. Then push the other side down on top of it and tuck in!

Jamie Oliver

Pancakes USA stylie

These American pancakes are great! Instead of being
thin and silky like French crêpes, they are wonderfully
fluffy and thick and can be made to perfection straight
away. Simple, simple, simple – my Jools goes mad for
them!

Serves 2–4
3 large eggs • 115g/4oz plain flour • 1 heaped
teaspoon baking powder • 140ml/5fl oz milk •
a pinch of salt

First separate the eggs, putting the whites into one bowl
and the yolks into another. Add the flour, baking powder
and milk to the yolks and mix to a smooth thick batter.
Whisk the whites with the salt until they form stiff
peaks. Fold into the batter – it is now ready to use.

Heat a good non-stick pan on a medium heat. Pour
some of your batter into the pan and fry for a couple
of minutes until it starts to look golden and firm. At
this point sprinkle your chosen flavouring (see opposite)
on to the uncooked side before loosening with a spatula
and flipping the pancake over. Continue frying until
both sides are golden.

You can make these pancakes large or small, to your
liking. You can serve them simply doused in maple
syrup and even with some butter or crème fraîche. Or
if you choose to sprinkle with a flavouring, try one of
these . . .

fresh corn from the cob • crispy bacon or pancetta •
blueberries • banana • stewed apple • grated chocolate •
anything else you can imagine . . .

Soft boiled egg with asparagus on toast

Serves 4

2 ripe plum tomatoes • sea salt and freshly ground
black pepper • extra virgin olive oil • 8 slices pancetta
or dry-cured smoky bacon • 4 large free-range eggs •
400g/14oz asparagus • 4 good slices of rustic
cottage-style bread • a knob of butter

Get some water boiling and your griddle pan on. Halve
your tomatoes and place on a roasting tray, cut side facing
up. Season, drizzle with a little oil and grill. When they
start to colour, lay your slices of pancetta next to them,
continue grilling until the pancetta is crisp and remove.

Carefully place your eggs and asparagus in the water
and boil for just under 4 minutes. Depending on the thickness of the asparagus, you may want to fish it out a little
earlier. Toast each piece of bread and put a slice on each
of the 4 plates. Remove your eggs and asparagus from
the water once cooked. In a bowl, toss the asparagus in
the butter to coat. Peel your soft-boiled eggs. To make it
really scrumptious get one half of tomato and rub and
squash it into your bread, then divide your asparagus on
top. Lay the pancetta over that and then top each carefully with an egg. Once secure, cut open the egg and allow
all the lovely yolk to dribble down through the asparagus
and on to the bread. Drizzle with olive oil and tuck in.

Long Lunches

Tray-baked lamb with aubergines, tomatoes, olives, garlic and mint oil

Serves 4
2 x 7-rib racks of lamb, preferably organic,
French-trimmed • 2 firm aubergines • 8 ripe plum
tomatoes • extra virgin olive oil • 8 cloves of garlic,
skin left on • dried oregano • sea salt and freshly
ground black pepper • optional: fresh basil or
marjoram • 1 large handful of fresh mint • a pinch
of sugar • good red wine vinegar

Preheat the oven to 200°C/400°F/gas 6. Criss-cross the
fat on the lamb – this will help it render and become
nice and crisp. Place to one side.

Slice your aubergines crossways into 2.5cm/1-inch
thick pieces and cut your tomatoes in half. Lightly brush
your aubergine slices all over with extra virgin olive oil,
then fry on both sides in a non-stick pan to give them
just a little colour. Remove the aubergines from the pan
and place on one side of a clean roasting tray. Put your
halved tomatoes and whole garlic cloves beside them
and sprinkle with a little oregano and seasoning. You
could always rip a little fresh basil or marjoram over the
tomatoes as well.

Season the lamb and fry in your non-stick pan until lightly golden on all sides. Drizzle with a little olive oil, then place the lamb skin-side up next to your aubergines and tomatoes and bake in the preheated oven for 30 minutes to retain a little pinkness – but you can always cook it to suit your taste. Remove from the oven and allow the lamb to rest for 5 minutes.

Now make some fantastic mint oil. Put the mint into either a pestle and mortar or a blender with a pinch each of salt and sugar, and blitz up until smooth. Add a couple of tablespoons of good red wine vinegar and loosen with 6 tablespoons of extra virgin olive oil. Season to taste and tweak with a little vinegar if need be. This is a fantastic sauce that is great drizzled over your veg and lamb. I like to cut my lamb in half between the ribs and then divide each half into 3 or 4 cutlets. There's always an extra rib, but that doesn't necessarily mean that someone else gets more meat than you.

PS: When you buy your racks of lamb, ask the butcher to 'French-trim' them, which means that all the bones are scraped clean – this looks nice and pretty and the meat cooks more easily too.

Good old steak and Guinness pie

This is nice and easy to make as all you have to do is put a puff pastry lid on top of a dish filled with your stewed meat. I never serve anything else with these pies but if you want to, boiled potatoes and steamed greens always hit the spot.

Serves 6

680g/1½lb stewing beef, diced • sea salt and freshly ground black pepper • 2 heaped tablespoons flour • olive oil • 1 onion, peeled and roughly chopped • 1 large carrot, peeled and roughly chopped • 4 sticks of celery, washed and roughly chopped • 2 parsnips, peeled and roughly chopped • 1 handful of fresh mixed herbs (rosemary, thyme and bay), leaves picked • 565ml/1 pint Guinness • 2 x 400g/14oz tins of tomatoes • 1 x 500g/1lb 2oz pack of puff pastry • 1 egg, beaten

Season your beef generously with salt and pepper, sprinkle with the flour and toss around until coated. Heat 2 or 3 lugs of olive oil in a large casserole-type pan and fry your meat, in 2 batches if need be, until golden brown. Add the onion and fry for 1 more minute, then add the carrot, celery, parsnips and herbs. Fry for a further 4 minutes then pour in your Guinness. Add the tinned tomatoes and bring to the boil. Stir around, then simmer for around 2 hours or until the meat is really tender. The sauce should be nice and thick with an intensely tasty flavour. Season. At this point you could serve it as a stew with mash, or it will keep really well for a good 5 days in the fridge (while improving in flavour at the same time).

To make the pies, preheat the oven to 190°C/375°F/gas 5. Put your meat filling into an appropriately-sized baking dish or dishes. I like to make small individual pies – any high-sided round ovenproof bowls are fine. Roll out your pastry, dusting with flour as you go, until 0.5cm/¼ inch thick. Cut out 6 circles about 1cm/½ inch bigger than the tops of your bowls. Brush the rims of your bowls with beaten egg, then place the pastry circles on top, squashing the excess pastry down the outside of the bowls to secure. Lightly score the top of the pastry in a criss-cross fashion and brush with more of the beaten egg. Bake in the middle of the preheated oven for 45 minutes until golden and bubbling.

Fantastic roasted chicken

This roast chicken is really tasty. The principle is very similar to the perfect roast chicken recipe in my first book, getting fantastic flavours right into the bird.

Serves 6
1.8kg/4lb chicken, preferably organic • 1 large lemon •
8 slices prosciutto or Parma ham, thinly sliced •
1–2 cloves of garlic, peeled and finely chopped •
2 good handfuls of fresh thyme, leaves picked and
finely chopped • salt and freshly ground black pepper •
115g/4oz or ½ pack of softened butter •
1kg/2lb 3oz potatoes, peeled and cut into chunks •
1 large celeriac, peeled

Preheat the oven and an appropriately sized roasting tray to 220°C/425°F/gas 7. Wash your chicken inside and out and pat dry with kitchen paper. Using your fingers, part the breast skin from the breast meat. It's important to try to push your hand gently down the breast, being careful not to rip the skin. With a peeler, remove and chop the fragrant yellow skin of the lemon, keeping the peeled lemon to one side. Then tear up your prosciutto and add to a bowl with the lemon skin, garlic and thyme. Season, and then scrunch it all into the butter. Push this into the space you have made between the meat and the skin – rub and massage any that's left over in and around the bird. It's all tasty stuff. I could tell you to tie the chicken up but I've decided it's a palaver and not worth it in this case. Slash the thigh meat to allow the heat to penetrate a little more, which makes it taste better. Cut the peeled lemon in half and push it into the cavity. Then put your chicken in the hot roasting tray and roast in the preheated oven for 25 minutes.

While the chicken is cooking, parboil the potatoes in salted water for 10 minutes and drain. Cut the celeriac into irregular chunks around the same size as the potatoes. Remove the chicken from the oven, by which time the tasty butter will have melted, flavoured and cooked out of the chicken into the bottom of the tray, awaiting your potatoes and celeriac. Normally I put a fork into the cavity of the chicken and lift it out of the tray for 20 seconds while I toss and coat the vegetables in the butter. Put the chicken back on top of the vegetables and cook for around 45 minutes. Leave to stand for 10 minutes. Once the meat and vegetables have been removed, a little light gravy can be made in the tray on the hob with a splash of wine and stock, a little simmering and scraping.

Toad in the hole

Serves 4
sunflower oil • 8 large good-quality sausages •
4 sprigs of fresh rosemary • 2 large red onions,
peeled and sliced • 2 cloves of garlic, peeled and
finely sliced • 2 knobs of butter • 6 tablespoons
balsamic vinegar • 1 level tablespoon
good-quality vegetable stock powder or
1 vegetable stock cube

For the batter
285ml/½ pint milk • 115g/4oz plain flour •
a pinch of salt • 3 eggs

Mix the batter ingredients together, and put to one side.
I like the batter to go huge so the key thing is to have
an appropriately-sized baking tin – the thinner the better
– as we need to get the oil smoking hot.

Put 1cm/just under ½ inch of sunflower oil into a
baking tin, then place this on the middle shelf of your
oven at its highest setting (240–250°C/475°F/gas 9). Place
a larger tray underneath it to catch any oil that over-
flows from the tin while cooking. When the oil is very
hot, add your sausages. Keep your eye on them and
allow them to colour until lightly golden.

At this point, take the tin out of the oven, being very
careful, and pour your batter over the sausages. Throw
a couple of sprigs of rosemary into the batter. It will
bubble and possibly even spit a little, so carefully put

the tin back in the oven, and close the door. Don't open it for at least 20 minutes, as Yorkshire puddings can be a bit temperamental when rising. Remove from the oven when golden and crisp.

For the onion gravy, simply fry off your onions and garlic in the butter on a medium heat for about 5 minutes until they go sweet and translucent. You could add a little thyme or rosemary if you like. Add the balsamic vinegar and allow it to cook down by half. At this point, I do cheat a little and add a stock cube or powder. You can get some good ones in the supermarkets now that aren't full of rubbish. Sprinkle this in and add a little water. Allow to simmer and you'll have a really tasty onion gravy. Serve at the table with your Toad in the Hole, mashed potatoes, greens and baked beans or maybe a green salad if you're feeling a little guilty!

Roasted fillet of beef rolled in herbs and porcini mushrooms and wrapped in prosciutto

As far as roasted meat goes, this is extremely fast and simple, yet decadently rich. One of the tricks, whether you buy it in a deli or a supermarket, is to ask them to slice your prosciutto and lay it side by side on to an A3 (ish) sized piece of waxed paper.

Serves 4
12–18 slices prosciutto or Parma ham • 3 cloves of garlic, peeled • 1 good handful of dried porcini, soaked in around 285ml/½ pint boiling water • 3 good knobs of butter • juice of ½ a lemon • sea salt and freshly ground black pepper • 900g/2lb fillet of beef (preferably from the middle, left whole) • 1 good handful of fresh rosemary and thyme, leaves picked and chopped • 2 glasses of red wine

Preheat your oven and an appropriately sized roasting tray to 230°C/450°F/gas 8. Make sure there are no gaps in between the laid-out slices of prosciutto. Chop one of the garlic cloves and fry with the soaked porcini mushrooms in 1 knob of butter for a minute. Then add half of the soaking water (make sure it is grit-free). Simmer slowly and reduce for around 5 minutes before stirring in a squeeze of lemon, the remaining 2 knobs of butter and seasoning. Rub your tasty and moist mushrooms over half of the laid-out prosciutto. Season your fillet of beef and roll it in the herbs. Place it on the mushroomy end of the prosciutto and slowly roll up the meat. Once the beef is rolled up, pull off the paper and push in the ends of the prosciutto to neaten. Lightly secure with 4 pieces of string. Chefs have a certain way of doing this, but as long as the string holds the meat together I don't care how you do it.

Place the fillet in the hot roasting tray with a couple of cloves of garlic and cook for 25–30 minutes (rare), 40 minutes (medium), 50 minutes (well-done) or 60 minutes (cremated!). Halfway through, add the wine to the tray. When the meat is done, remove it to a chopping board and leave it to rest for 5 minutes. Pour any juices back into the roasting tray. Simmer the juices on the hob, scraping all the goodness from the sides of the tray. Remove from the heat and serve as a light red wine gravy. Slice the fillet as thick or as thin as you like and serve with some potatoes or some gorgeous greens. I like to reserve a little of the cooked porcini to serve with my greens.

Unbelievable roast pork with stuffed apples and parsnips

As usual I was mucking about, trying to reinvent the apple sauce and roast pork story. I roasted everything in the pan together, and the flavours were absolutely amazing. What a brilliant way to eat apples with pork rather than having boring old apple sauce.

Serves 6

½ a pork loin, rib-end • 6 large parsnips, peeled and cut lengthways • 6 small red onions, peeled • sea salt and freshly ground black pepper • 2 handfuls of fresh sage, leaves picked • 1 heaped teaspoon ground allspice • ½ a nutmeg, grated • 2 cloves of garlic, peeled • zest of 1 orange • 150g/5½oz butter, softened • 6 good eating apples

Preheat your oven to 220°C/425°F/gas 7. Sometimes the fat in pork can be too thick and never goes crisp. So ask your butcher to score through the skin about 1cm/½ inch apart then remove it from the loin. You want to try to leave about 0.5cm/¼ inch of fat on the loin, and score this across so it goes nice and crisp when you cook it. Season the skin well and place on a tray in the oven to start crackling – this will take around 15–20 minutes, depending on how moist the skin is. Remove when golden and crisp and put to one side. Meanwhile parboil your parsnips and red onions in boiling, salted water for about 5 minutes.

In a pestle and mortar (or in a metal bowl using the end of a rolling pin) bash up the sage, allspice, nutmeg, garlic and orange zest with a good pinch of salt and pepper until you have a fine powder. Put the mixture into a bowl with your butter, then mix it all up well. Run a knife around the middle of each apple – this will stop them bursting when they cook. Remove the core with a peeler without piercing right through the apple and discard. Pack your flavoured butter into the cavity of each apple where the core was – any excess butter can be smeared all over the pork loin. Place the apples in the tray, butter side facing down, with the parboiled parsnips and red onions. Put the pork on top and place in the oven for half an hour, then take the tray out of the oven, remove the pork to a plate and carefully toss the onion and parsnips in all the lovely cooking juices, trying not to disrupt the apples. Put the pork back on top and continue cooking for half an hour at 180°C/350°F/gas 4 until nice and golden. When done, remove the pork from the oven and allow to rest for 5 minutes before slicing. Turn the oven off, but keep the veggies and crackling warm in the oven until you're ready to serve.

Carve the pork and divide between your 6 plates with the veggies and an apple each.

Try this: Steam yourself some nice greens, toss them in the buttery juices from the roasting tray and serve along-side the pork.

Braised five-hour lamb with wine, veg and all that

This is a real hearty and trouble-free dinner. There's barely any preparation, just a nice long cooking time which will reward you with the most tender meat and tasty sauce. Large legs of lamb are ideal for this dish as they benefit from slow cooking. If using a smaller leg of spring lamb then consider cooking for an hour less.

Serves 6

1 large leg of lamb • salt and freshly ground black pepper • olive oil • 6 rashers of thick streaky bacon • 3 red onions, peeled and quartered • 3 cloves of garlic, peeled and sliced • 2 good handfuls of mixed fresh herbs (thyme, rosemary, bay) • 4 large potatoes, peeled and cut into chunks • 1 celeriac, peeled and cut into chunks • 6 large carrots, scrubbed and halved • 3 parsnips, scrubbed and halved • 1 bottle of white wine

Preheat the oven to 170°C/325°F/gas 3. In a large casserole pot or a deep-sided roasting tray, fry your well-seasoned lamb in a couple of good lugs of olive oil until brown on all sides. Add the bacon, onions and garlic and continue to fry for 3 more minutes. Throw in your herbs and veg, pour in your wine plus an equivalent amount of water, bring to the boil, and tightly cover with kitchen foil. Bake in the preheated oven for

5 hours until tender, seasoning the cooking liquor to taste. To serve, pull away a nice portion of meat, take a selection of veg and serve with some crusty bread to mop up the gravy.

Onion gravy

No Sunday lunch is complete without gravy. Here's a simple onion gravy that goes with almost everything but is particularly good with sausages and mash.

4 medium red onions, peeled and finely sliced •
olive oil • 5 tablespoons balsamic or red wine vinegar •
40g/1½oz butter • 2 beef or chicken stock cubes

Fry the onions – really slowly – in a little oil, covered, for about 15 minutes until soft. Remove the lid, turn the heat up, and as soon as the onions become golden brown, pour in the vinegar and boil until it almost disappears. Turn the heat down again, add the butter, crumble in your stock cubes and 565ml/1 pint of water and stir well. Let this simmer until you have a nice gravy consistency then serve while piping hot.

Fish Suppers

Magnificent roasted monkfish

The whole idea behind this recipe was to be able to make something really quick and ultra-tasty and present it in a way that looked like you'd been working for hours on it. As monkfish comes in different sizes, feel free to do individual 200g/7oz fillets or to cook a whole larger fillet and divide it up once cooked. So, here goes.

Serves 4
1 small jar of sun-dried tomatoes in oil • 2 large
handfuls of fresh basil • olive oil • 16–20 slices
of Parma ham • 4 x 200g/7oz monkfish tail fillets,
trimmed • sea salt and freshly ground black pepper •
optional: balsamic vinegar and rocket, to serve

Preheat the oven to 200°C/400°F/gas 6. Place your sun-dried tomatoes and half their flavoursome preserving oil in a Magimix food processor with all your basil and blend until smooth. While blending, I add the remaining preserving oil to the paste until it's nice and spreadable. Sometimes even a dash of balsamic vinegar is quite nice to flavour and loosen.

You are going to need 4 A4-sized pieces of grease-proof paper. Rub some olive oil over each piece of greaseproof paper and lay about 4 slices of Parma ham snugly next to each other, on each piece of paper. Divide your paste into 4, smearing each part evenly over the ham. Then place your monkfish fillets at one end, season, and, using the greaseproof paper, fold and roll up. Remove the greaseproof paper and carefully move to an oiled baking tray or dish, then roast in the preheated oven for 15–20 minutes.

I like to slice the fish up and serve it with some really buttery mashed potato, thinned down with lots of milk. And maybe drizzle a little balsamic vinegar over the fish, and scatter a little rocket over the whole plate.

Fantastic fish pie

The whole fish pie thing is one of the most homely, comforting and moreish dinners I can think of. This is a cracking recipe which does it for me.

Serves 6

5 large potatoes, peeled and diced into 2.5cm/1 inch squares • salt and freshly ground black pepper • 2 free-range eggs • 2 large handfuls of fresh spinach • 1 onion, finely chopped • 1 carrot, halved and finely chopped • extra virgin olive oil • approx. 285ml/ ½ pint double cream • 2 good handfuls of grated mature Cheddar or Parmesan cheese • juice of 1 lemon • 1 heaped teaspoon English mustard • 1 large handful of flat-leaf parsley, finely chopped • 455g/1lb haddock or cod fillet, skin removed, pin-boned and sliced into strips • nutmeg (optional)

Preheat the oven to 230°C/450°F/gas 8. Put the potatoes into salted boiling water and bring back to the boil for 2 minutes. Carefully add the eggs to the pan and cook for a further 8 minutes until hard-boiled, by which time the potatoes should also be cooked. At the same time, steam the spinach in a colander above the pan. This will only take a minute. When the spinach is done, remove from the colander and gently squeeze any excess moisture away. Then drain the potatoes in the colander. Remove the eggs, cool under cold water, then peel and quarter them. Place to one side.

In a separate pan slowly fry the onion and carrot in a little olive oil for about 5 minutes, then add the double cream and bring just to the boil. Remove from the heat and add the cheese, lemon juice, mustard and parsley. Put the spinach, fish and eggs into an appropriately sized earthenware dish and mix together, pouring over the creamy vegetable sauce. The cooked potatoes should be drained and mashed – add a bit of olive oil, salt, pepper and a touch of nutmeg if you like. Spread on top of the fish. Don't bother piping it to make it look pretty – it's a homely hearty thing. Place in the oven for about 25–30 minutes until the potatoes are golden. Serve with some nice peas or greens, not forgetting your baked beans and tomato ketchup. Tacky but tasty and that's what I like.

Baked trout and potatoes with a crème fraîche, walnut and horseradish sauce

Trout is a fantastic and readily available fish. The combination of hot horseradish, nutty walnuts and creamy crème fraîche goes incredibly well with trout as well as with the more obvious beef and lamb.

Serves 4

455g/1lb potatoes, peeled and finely sliced • olive oil • salt and freshly ground black pepper • 4 whole trout, approx. 400–455g/14oz–1lb each, gutted and scaled • 1 heaped tablespoon grated fresh horseradish • 255g/9oz crème fraîche • 2 handfuls of fresh walnuts, shelled and crushed • juice of 1 lemon

Optional

a little fresh thyme, leaves picked • 1 lemon, sliced

Preheat the oven to 240°C/475°F/gas 9. Dry your sliced potatoes with kitchen paper and lightly coat in olive oil. Season and place in a single layer in a large roasting tray. Place on a low oven shelf and roast for around 15 minutes, until crisp and golden. Meanwhile pat the trout dry, then with a sharp knife slash each fish at an angle on both sides – this will allow the heat and seasoning to penetrate. Rub with olive oil and seasoning. For extra flavour you can stuff the fish with fragrant herbs. I like to use thyme with some lemon slices too. This should only take a couple of minutes. Cook for around 12 minutes at the top of the oven until crisp and golden.

While the fish and potatoes are cooking make your sauce. Fresh horseradish, which you should peel and grate, is nicer, but you can also use the creamed horse-radish bought in jars. Not quite as hot but still tasty. Mix the horseradish in a bowl with the crème fraîche and the walnuts and season well. Squeeze over some lemon juice to taste.

Serve the fish and potatoes side by side with a good dollop of the crème fraîche sauce. Really nice with a green salad, some buttered bread and a glass of beer.

Roasted slashed fillet of sea bass stuffed with herbs, baked on mushroom potatoes with salsa verde – à la Tony Blair

I cooked this for Tony Blair and the Italian prime minister at their British/Italian summit. It went down a treat so I thought I'd include it here. This is a really great way to cook sea bass. Try to get the fattest bass fillets you can find. Failing that, royal bream is fantastic cooked this way too.

Serves 4
4 x 225g/8oz sea bass fillets • 1 handful of mixed herbs (green or purple basil, flat-leaf parsley, thyme), roughly chopped • 1kg/2lb 3oz potatoes, scrubbed • olive oil • 2 cloves of garlic, finely chopped • salt and freshly ground black pepper • 3 knobs of butter • 455g/1lb mixed, preferably wild, mushrooms, torn • 3 lemons

For the salsa verde
2 cloves of garlic, peeled • 1 small handful of capers • 1 small handful of pickled gherkins (the ones in sweet vinegar) • 6 anchovy fillets • 2 large handfuls of flat-leaf parsley, leaves picked • 1 bunch of fresh basil, leaves picked • 1 handful of fresh mint, leaves picked • 1 tablespoon Dijon mustard • 3 tablespoons red wine vinegar • approx. 120ml/8 tablespoons of your best olive oil • sea salt and freshly ground black pepper

Preheat the oven to 240°C/475°F/gas 9. Put a bit of greaseproof paper on the bottom of a baking tray, rubbed with olive oil. Slash the fish fillets about half-way down and stuff the slashes with the herbs. Slice the potatoes lengthways, just under 1cm/½ inch thick. Dry them off with kitchen paper and very lightly coat them in olive oil. Mix in half of your garlic, season with salt and pepper, then lay them out in one layer on the tray. Cook the potatoes in the oven for around 15 minutes until just cooked. Remove and put to one side.

Put the rest of the garlic into a pan with 2 good knobs of butter and a lug of olive oil. Fry your mixed mushrooms and season until tasty. If water comes out of them just continue cooking until it evaporates. Take the pan off the heat, squeeze in the juice from 1 lemon and stir in another knob of butter. Now scatter the mushrooms over the potatoes and kind of rub them in on top, underneath, all over. Place your sea bass fillets on top. Now bake in the oven for 12–15 minutes, depending on the thickness of your fish.

While your fish is baking, prepare the salsa verde. Finely chop the first seven ingredients and put them into a bowl. Add the mustard and red wine vinegar, then slowly stir in the olive oil. Balance the flavours with freshly ground black pepper and, if necessary, sea salt and a little more red wine vinegar.

When the fish is cooked, remove the tray from the oven, put some kitchen foil over the top and let it sit for about 5 minutes, during which time all the lovely juices will run out into the potatoes. Serve it with the salsa verde, half a lemon each and a glass of crisp white wine.

Parmesan fish fillets with avocado and cress salad

Serves 1

2 tablespoons flour • salt and freshly ground black pepper • 170g/6oz white fish fillets, skin removed • 1 egg, beaten • 55g/2oz freshly grated Parmesan cheese • olive oil • ½ a fresh red chilli, deseeded and finely chopped • 1 ripe avocado, peeled and sliced lengthways • 1 punnet of cress • 1 tablespoon extra virgin olive oil • juice of ½ a lemon

Get a frying pan really hot. Season the flour with salt and pepper. Dust the fish fillets with the seasoned flour, then dip into the egg and press into the grated Parmesan, making sure the fish is nicely covered. Add a little olive oil to the hot pan, and fry the fish fillets for a couple of minutes on each side until golden brown. Throw in the chilli. Mix together the avocado and cress with the extra virgin olive oil and lemon juice, and put on your plate with your fish fillets.

Drinks

Sidecar

This is a superb little cocktail and the recipe is from Tony Debok at a bar called Daddy-O in New York. Definitely one to try.

Serves 1 (large)
3 tablespoons caster sugar • 55ml/2fl oz good brandy •
20–25ml/¾fl oz Cointreau • 2 or 3 fresh limes, juiced
• sugar and lime rind, to serve

First stir 3 tablespoons of sugar and 3 tablespoons of boiling water together until dissolved, then add the brandy, Cointreau and lime juice. Add some ice and shake well. Taste a little – you may want to add some more lime to give it an edge. Serve up in a martini glass with a sugar rim and a lime twist.

Margarita

Serves 1

2 shots of tequila • 1 shot of Cointreau • 1 shot of freshly squeezed lime juice • salt and lime wedge, to serve

Put all the ingredients into a shaker. Shake well and serve in a martini glass with a salt rim and a split lime wedge.

On the Sidelines

Minty mushy peas

This is a fantastic recipe which is so quick and so simple and uses our reliable friends the frozen peas, which work really well here. Great with fish, meat or even as a vegetarian dish with a big dollop of butter on top.

Serves 4–6
2 medium-sized potatoes, peeled and finely diced •
1kg/2lb 3oz frozen peas • 1 handful of fresh mint,
leaves picked • 3 large knobs of butter • sea salt
and freshly ground black pepper

Boil the potatoes in salted boiling water until nearly tender. Add your peas to the pan and then after 2 minutes of boiling add the mint. After another minute, drain everything into a colander. Leave for 1 minute to steam, then put everything back into the pan and mash with a potato masher. You can do this in a Magimix food processor as well – just pulse it until smooth. Whether mashing or pulsing, when it's done add your butter and season very carefully to taste.

Baked new potatoes with sea salt and rosemary

Serves 4–6
1kg/2lb 3oz Jersey Royals • 1 tablespoon olive oil •
Maldon sea salt and freshly ground black pepper •
2 sprigs of rosemary, leaves picked and bashed

Wash your potatoes and parboil until almost tender. When done, drain them, drizzle with just a little touch of olive oil and roll in a tablespoon of Maldon sea salt, a little freshly ground black pepper and the rosemary. Preheat the oven to 220°C/425°F/gas 7. Put the potatoes in a roasting tray and cook in the oven for 25 minutes until golden. Or wrap them in tin-foil and throw them on the barbie for the same amount of time.

Baked carrots with cumin, thyme, butter and Chardonnay

I love this dish made with baby carrots, but feel free to use fat old ones sliced at an angle if you please. Butter and wine make a fantastic sauce which just makes it for me. Serve with anything you like.

Serves 4
455g/1lb baby carrots, preferably organic, scrubbed
and left whole • ½ teaspoon cumin seeds, crushed •
1 handful of fresh thyme leaves • 4 knobs of butter •

1 glass of Chardonnay • salt and freshly ground
black pepper

Preheat the oven to 220°C/425°F/gas 7. Tear off around a metre and a half (5ft) of kitchen foil and fold it in half to give you double thickness. Place everything but the wine and seasoning in the middle of the foil. Bring up the sides and pour in the white wine. Season well. Fold or scrunch the foil together to seal. Cook in the preheated oven for 45 minutes until the carrots are tender. You may need to cook for longer if the carrots are bigger than baby ones.

Slow-roasted balsamic tomatoes with baby leeks and basil

This is one of those recipes that, apart from being damn tasty, is kind of slapdash but so easy to make and consistently good. You can really get some mileage out of it. The key things are to get yourself some best-quality plum tomatoes and buy some cheap balsamic vinegar, as you'll be using a lot of it.

Serves 6
12 plum tomatoes • 4 cloves of garlic, peeled and
finely sliced • 1 handful of fresh basil, leaves picked
and torn up • 12 fresh bay leaves • 12 baby leeks,
trimmed and washed • sea salt and freshly ground
black pepper • 200ml/7fl oz cheap balsamic vinegar •
2 tablespoons extra virgin olive oil

Preheat the oven to 170°C/325°F/gas 3.

Score the tops of the tomatoes with a cross. Take an earthenware dish that the tomatoes will fit snugly into, and sprinkle the garlic and basil all over the bottom of it. Stand the tomatoes next to each other in the tray, on top of the garlic and basil, then push the bay leaves well into the scores in the tomatoes and season well. Lay the leeks on a board and sprinkle generously with salt and pepper. Using a rolling pin, press down on top of the leeks to really squeeze the seasoning into them. This will also loosen their texture. Weave the leeks in and around the tomatoes. Pour over the balsamic vinegar, drizzle over the olive oil, and bake in the preheated oven for an hour. Before serving, remove the bay leaves.

Try this: These tomatoes are great served as a vegetable dish, or as part of a warm salad. Also good as a base for soup, puréed to make a sauce or served over pasta.

Alfresco Food

Rosemary skewered monkfish with pancetta and bread

This is a forever-winning combo that involves the slightly unusual marriage between meat and fish. It works out pretty cost-effective as well, because you're using less fish than you normally would and you're actually making it taste a lot more interesting too. Give it a bash.

Serves 4

455g/1lb trimmed monkfish tail or any meaty white fish • 1½ ciabatta loaves, crusts removed • 4 x 25cm/10 inch fresh rosemary twigs • 1 clove of garlic, peeled • extra virgin olive oil • sea salt and freshly ground black pepper • 12 rashers of pancetta or smoked streaky bacon • 1–2 tablespoons good balsamic vinegar

Preheat the oven to 220°C/425°F/gas 7. Cut the monkfish into 2.5cm/1-inch dice and add to a bowl with the ciabatta, ripped up into similar-sized pieces. Keeping the top 5cm/2 inches of rosemary leaves, run your thumb and forefinger down the length of the stalk, removing all the leaves. Throw these into a pestle and mortar and bash up with the garlic. Then stir in 5 or 6 tablespoons of extra virgin olive oil. Pour this over your monkfish and bread and toss around.

Now begin to skewer the kebabs. At an angle, slice the tip off the rosemary stalks, so they are sharp. Put a piece of monkfish on first, then bread, and repeat until you have about 3 pieces of monkfish and about 3 pieces of bread on each kebab and lightly season. Loosely wrap 3 pieces of pancetta round each kebab, weaving it in and around the fish and the bread. Place the kebabs on a roasting tray, sprinkle with any leftover oil and rosemary, and bake in the preheated oven for 15–20 minutes, until the bread is crisp and golden. Drizzle a little balsamic vinegar over each piece of monkfish, then a little extra olive oil and any juice from the tray. Serve simply with a good salad. Happy days!

Chargrilled marinated vegetables

The first time I ever made this was at the Neal Street
Restaurant, and about two years later, when I was at
the River Café, Rose Gray showed me her way of doing
it. She inspired me to think of grilling as a really excit-
ing way to prepare vegetables.

Serves 4–6
2 red peppers • 2 yellow peppers • 2 medium
courgettes • 1 bulb of fennel • 1 aubergine • 8 baby
leeks • sea salt and freshly ground black pepper •
extra virgin olive oil • 1 large bunch of fresh basil,
leaves picked • 2 tablespoons herb or white wine
vinegar • 1 clove of garlic

Wash all your vegetables. Heat the barbecue or a griddle
pan, put your whole peppers on it, and get them really
black on all sides. While still hot, put them in a bowl,
cover with clingfilm and leave to cool.

Slice your courgettes lengthways about 0.5cm / ¼ inch
thick and do the same with your fennel, reserving the
herby tops. Grill the courgette and fennel together on
the griddle pan for about a minute on each side or until
nicely charred. You don't want them too black or too
raw. Remove to a clean tea towel in one layer, making
sure they don't sit on top of each other, otherwise they
will steam and go soggy.

Cut the aubergine across into slices 1cm / ½ inch
thick. Every now and again you get an aubergine that

is really seedy – if this happens, it will be bitter and no good, so throw it away and get yourself another one. Chargrill the aubergine slices, turning them 4 times until nicely marked, then remove to the tea towel.

Boil the baby leeks in salted water until they're just cooked. Then drain, rub with a little olive oil, and chargrill them quickly until lightly marked.

Peel the peppers but don't hold them under the tap as all the sweet fantastic flavour will go down the drain. Carefully rub off the black skin, then remove the stalk and pips and tear the peppers up into large strips. Now put all the vegetables into a large bowl.

Take about a quarter of your basil leaves and bash them in a pestle and mortar with a good pinch of seasoning until you have a smooth pulp. Add about 8 tablespoons of extra virgin olive oil and the vinegar, to taste. Pour this over the vegetables and toss quickly so that everything gets coated in the lovely basil oil, then throw in the remaining whole basil leaves. Slice the garlic really thinly to give you a delicate flavour and add to the bowl with the fennel tops. Mix everything together, and serve on a large plate at room temperature. Great with any grilled fish or meat, or as part of an antipasti plate with some toasted bruschetta and some fresh buffalo mozzarella.

Broad bean and crispy pancetta salad with a pea, pecorino and mint dressing

Even though this salad's really simple and really tasty, it's also quite a brave dish because it hasn't got lots of leaves everywhere – just some beautiful ingredients put together with a little common sense. It's one of those combos that makes the back of your mouth juice up when you think about it. Ideally use young peas and broad beans when they're in season. If they're a little older then take the skins off the beans, and if the peas are large it doesn't really matter as you'll be mushing them up anyway.

Serves 4

1 clove of garlic, peeled and left whole • 300g/10½oz podded broad beans • 8 slices of pancetta or smoked streaky bacon • 1 handful of whole blanched almonds • 150g/5½oz podded fresh peas • 70g/2½oz Pecorino or Parmesan cheese, or a mixture of both, grated • 1 handful of fresh mint, leaves picked • 8 tablespoons extra virgin olive oil • juice of 1–2 lemons • sea salt and freshly ground black pepper

Bring a pot to the boil, half-filled with water, but with no salt as this makes broad beans and peas toughen. Add your garlic and allow the water to boil for a couple of minutes before adding the broad beans. Cook for around 3–5 minutes, depending on how young the beans are. Simply taste one to check. If you feel the skins are a little tough, which they can be sometimes, let them cool a little and then you can peel them very quickly by pinching and squeezing the bean out. Throw the skins away, and keep the garlic clove to one side. Place your pancetta on a baking tray, with the almonds spread out next to it. Place in a hot oven at 250°C/475°F/gas 9 – keeping an eye on the almonds to make sure they don't colour too much. You should be able to crisp up the pancetta at the same time as toasting the almonds, but simply remove one or the other if it is getting too far ahead.

To make the dressing, put your raw podded peas and the soft, boiled garlic clove into a pestle and mortar or a Magimix and bash or blitz until smooth. Add the cheese and most of the mint and stir or pulse to make a smooth paste. You want to turn this into a thick dressing, so add the olive oil and 4–5 tablespoons of lemon juice, to your preference. Season to taste – it should have an amazing flavour of sweet peas, twangy lemon, fragrant mint and a softness and roundness from the cheese. A balance is good, but you should also trust your own personal judgement – I generally like mine to be a bit more lemony, to cut through the smokiness of the pancetta.

Mix the dressing with the broad beans and sprinkle this over 4 plates. Crumble the pancetta over, followed by a sprinkling of the almonds, which can be crushed or bashed up a little. Tear a little mint over the top with a little shaved Parmesan if you like.

Couscous with grilled summer vegetables and loadsa herbs

This couscous recipe is quite a bit different from the norm because instead of boiling or steaming the couscous you just feed it from raw with a really tasty dressing. This means it keeps a slight bite which I think is more interesting for a salad.

Serves 4

255g/9oz couscous • 285ml/½ pint cold water •
3 red peppers • 1 handful of asparagus, trimmed and peeled if need be • 2 or 3 small firm courgettes/patty pans, sliced • 1 small bunch of spring onions, trimmed and finely sliced • 2–4 fresh red chillies, deseeded and finely sliced • 3 good handfuls of mixed fresh herbs (basil, coriander, mint, flat-leaf parsley) • salt and freshly ground black pepper • red wine vinegar

For the dressing

2 tablespoons lemon juice • 5 tablespoons olive oil •
salt and freshly ground black pepper, to taste

Place the couscous in a bowl with the cold water. This will start to soften the couscous and you will see the water disappear as it soaks in. While the couscous is softening, we need to blacken the peppers. I do this by placing the peppers directly on to the naked flame of my gas hob. If you don't have gas, then blacken under the grill. Both ways you need to blacken the peppers on all sides, so turn when need be. When fully blackened, place in a sandwich bag, wrap in clingfilm or cover in a bowl for 5 minutes until cool. This will steam the skins and make peeling and deseeding easier. Remove the skins and seeds and roughly chop.

On a very hot ridged grill pan, lightly char the asparagus and courgettes or patty pans on both sides then toss them into the bowl of couscous with the peppers, spring onions, chillies and ripped-up herbs. Mix well. Now put all your dressing ingredients into a jam jar, tighten the lid and shake up. Add the dressing to the couscous and toss well. Finally, taste and season with salt and pepper and a couple of dribbles of red wine vinegar for a slight twang. It's a beautiful thing.

Kebabs

LAMB

Serves 6–8

500g/1lb 2oz lamb, trimmed and cut into 2.5cm/ 1-inch cubes • 6–8 skewers or sticks of fresh rosemary, lower leaves removed, tips kept on • 2 red onions, peeled and quartered • 2 red peppers, deseeded and cut into 2.5cm/1-inch pieces

For the marinade

1 tablespoon smoked paprika • 2 cloves • ½ teaspoon cumin seeds • 2 teaspoons coriander seeds • sea salt and freshly ground black pepper • olive oil

First bash up all the spices in a pestle and mortar until fine, then mix with the oil to make a thick marinade paste. Put the lamb pieces into a bowl and cover with the marinade. Let them sit there for half an hour to an hour. Then, using the rosemary sticks or skewers, spike each piece of meat alternately with red onion and peppers. Grill for around 5 minutes, turning regularly, to give you nicely charred meat on the outside with juicy pink on the inside. Allow to rest for a few minutes – that is, if you can stop yourself eating them straight away!

CHICKEN

Serves 6–8

500g/1lb 2oz free-range boneless chicken breasts •
4 courgettes, sliced very thinly lengthways •
6–8 skewers or sticks of fresh rosemary, lower
leaves removed, tips kept on

For the marinade

1 handful of fresh coriander • 1 handful of fresh mint •
3 cloves of garlic • 6 spring onions • 1 red chilli •
zest and juice of 1 lemon • sea salt and freshly
ground black pepper • olive oil

Cut the chicken into 2.5cm/1-inch cubes and place in a bowl. Blanch the courgette strips in salted boiling water for 30 seconds then drain and allow to cool. Blitz all the marinade ingredients except the olive oil in a food processor, then loosen to a paste with a little olive oil. Add the marinade to the chicken pieces and mix well. Allow to sit for up to an hour. Then weave the courgette strips in between the chicken pieces on the rosemary sticks or skewers. Grill for around 5 minutes, turning regularly, until cooked. Feel free to cut a piece open to check if they're done.

FISH

Serves 6–8

500g/1lb 2oz monkfish tail (or cod or haddock), trimmed of all skin and bone and cut into 2.5cm/ 1-inch cubes • 6–8 skewers or sticks of fresh rosemary, lower leaves removed, tips kept on • 255g/9oz boiled new potatoes, halved

For the marinade

2 thumb-sized pieces of fresh ginger, thinly sliced • juice and zest of 1 lemon • 1 teaspoon turmeric • 2 cloves of garlic • 2 dried chillies, crumbled • 1 hand-ful of fresh mint • 4 tablespoons natural yoghurt

Put all the marinade ingredients except the yoghurt into a food processor and blitz until smooth. Stir in the yoghurt. Using the skewers or rosemary sticks, skewer the fish alternately with the new potatoes. Drizzle with the marinade and grill for 2 minutes each side.

Mozzarella and grilled chilli salad

Another great salad that can get away with being part of an antipasti selection as well as a main course salad or sandwich filling. Simple flavours again: it's all based around the milky soft mozzarella and the slightly more refined heat of the grilled chilli. If possible try to buy buffalo mozzarella, as it's made out of buffalo milk which makes the cheese far more tasty and delicate in both texture and taste. The salad doesn't work nearly as well with that chewy horrible stuff that is used on pizzas.

I normally use 1 fresh red chilli to every ball of mozzarella, but do use more or less as you please. Prick the chillies with a knife, otherwise they can puff up and explode in your face, and place them straight on to the naked flame if you have a gas hob. If you don't have gas, put them in a pan on the highest setting of your electric hob. Both ways you need to blacken the chillies on all sides, so turn when need be. When fully blackened, place in a sandwich bag, wrap in clingfilm or cover in a bowl for 5 minutes until cool. This will steam the skins and make peeling and deseeding easier.

While the chillies are steaming, gently rip up your mozzarella into 4 or 5 pieces and randomly place on a large plate. Peel and deseed the chillies and slice lengthways as thinly as you like. It's quite important to scatter them evenly over the mozzarella and very important to wash your hands after doing so before you rub your eyes or anything else! Now rip up some purple and green basil over the top, and sprinkle with sea salt and freshly ground black pepper. Add a little squeeze of lemon juice and a generous lug of olive oil. Nice one.

Scrummy warm rocket salad

Warm salads can be blooming amazing or a complete disaster. First, you have got to get your hungry guests around the table before you plate up, so as soon as their bums are on the chairs, you are tossing the warm ingredients in with the rocket leaves. Boom, boom, boom on a plate and it's in front of them.

Serves 4

Peel, halve and quarter 2 medium red onions, then quarter again, to give you 8 pieces from each onion. Heat a frying pan and fry off 8 whole rashers of pancetta or smoked streaky bacon until crisp. Remove, add a couple of lugs of olive oil to the pan, and add 4 sprigs of thyme, the onions and a good handful of pinenuts with a pinch of salt. Toss around and fry on a medium heat for about 5 minutes until caramelized and sweet (not black!). Put your pancetta or bacon back into the pan, toss around, then throw everything into a salad bowl with 4 big handfuls of rocket or any nice salad leaves. Drizzle generously with balsamic vinegar – this will make a natural dressing as it mixes with the olive oil. Serve with some shaved Parmesan over the top – you can use a potato peeler to do this. Munch away.

Puds

Fruit cobbler

This is a fantastic American recipe equivalent to our crumble. Particularly good with strawberries and rhubarb, but you can use any fruit combo you like; about 680g/1½lb of fruit should do it.

Serves 6

For the fruit

2 apricots, stoned and sliced • 1 pear, cored and thickly sliced • 1 punnet of blackberries • 1 punnet of blueberries • 1 punnet of raspberries • ½ an apple, grated • 5 tablespoons sugar • a good glug of balsamic vinegar

For the topping

6 heaped tablespoons butter, chilled • 225g/8oz self-raising flour • 70g/2½oz sugar • a large pinch of salt • 130ml/4½fl oz buttermilk • a little extra sugar for dusting

Preheat the oven to 190°C/375°F/gas 5. Put the fruit into a pan with the sugar and the balsamic vinegar, put the pan over the heat, and cook gently until the juices begin to run from the berries. Pour into an ovenproof dish.

Meanwhile make the topping. Rub the cold butter into the flour until the mixture resembles fine bread-crumbs. Add the sugar and salt, stir well, then add the buttermilk to form a loose scone-type mixture. Spoon this over the hot fruit (to get a cobbled effect, flick balls of dough randomly over the fruit), sprinkle with a little caster sugar, and bake in your preheated oven for 30 minutes until golden brown. Serve with vanilla ice cream.

Campari and passionfruit sorbet

Serves 4
285ml / ½ pint water • 200g/7oz sugar •
15 passionfruit • 1 wine glass of Campari

Place the water and sugar in a pan, bring to the boil and simmer for 5 minutes. Remove from the heat and allow to cool for a while. Halve your passionfruit and scoop out the flesh, seeds and juice using a spoon. Stir this up – you can pass it through a coarse sieve to remove the seeds, but quite frankly I think that's a palaver. I like the seeds. Mix the passionfruit with the Campari and sugar syrup in a plastic tub or earthenware dish and place in the freezer. Generally, sorbet takes 2 hours to set. Try to stir it around every half an hour if you remember. Serve on its own, with some seasonal fruit, or in a cone with some vanilla ice-cream.

Yoghurt with blueberry jam and elderflower cordial

This is a fantastic quick recipe for those days when you don't want to spend ages knocking up a dessert. Or it can be a really good intermediate palate cleanser before your main course. It can be made with any jam you like, but blueberry jam is particularly tasty. Try strawberry or raspberry too.

Serves 4
1 x 500g/1lb 2oz pot of good-quality Greek
or natural yoghurt • 4 tablespoons blueberry
jam • 8 tablespoons elderflower cordial •
4 sprigs of fresh mint

Divide your yoghurt between 4 dessert bowls or small glasses. Spoon over your blueberry jam, cover with your elderflower cordial, and top with a sprig of mint.

Lovely lemon curdy pud

This is really tasty and dead easy to make – my sister Anna loves it! It looks good cooked in a Pyrex dish, as it goes into layers as it cooks, with a sort of lemon curdy custard at the bottom and a spongy meringuey top. Mmmmmmm . . . very delicious!

Serves 4
55g/2oz butter • 115g/4oz sugar (vanilla sugar is nice) • grated rind and juice of 1 lemon • 2 large eggs, separated • 55g/2oz self-raising flour • 285ml/½ pint milk

Preheat the oven to 200°C/400°F/gas 6. Cream the butter, sugar and lemon rind in a mixing bowl. Add the egg yolks and flour and beat in, then add the milk and 3 tablespoons of lemon juice and mix well.

Whisk the egg whites in a separate bowl until stiff, then add the rest of the mixture. Mix it all well but don't over-mix it; you don't want the air to come out of the egg whites. Pour into a buttered ovenproof dish, stand the dish in a roasting tin about a third full of water, then bake in your preheated oven for about 45 minutes until the top is set and spongy and it's a nice golden colour.

Party cake

3 rounded tablespoons cocoa powder • 200g/7oz
caster sugar • 200g/7oz butter • 3 large eggs,
preferably free-range • 200g/7oz self-raising flour,
sifted • 1 rounded teaspoon baking powder •
1 handful of flaked almonds • 200ml/7fl oz double
cream • 1 large handful of raspberries • 1 large
handful of strawberries

For the chocolate topping
100g/3¾oz butter • 100g/3¾oz best cooking
chocolate • 100g/3¾oz icing sugar •
3 tablespoons milk

Preheat the oven to 180°C/350°F/gas 4. Line the bases
of 2 x 20cm/8-inch cake tins with greased greaseproof
paper. Mix the cocoa powder with 4 tablespoons of
boiling water until smooth. In a separate bowl, beat
the sugar and butter until fluffy, add the cocoa mixture,
eggs, flour and baking powder. Mix well, then fold in
the nuts. Divide the mixture between the tins. Bake for
about 25 minutes. When cooked, allow to cool then
remove from the tins.

Melt the chocolate topping ingredients in a bowl over
some lightly simmering water. Stir until blended well and
allow to cool. Whip the double cream to soft peaks
and sweeten with a little sugar to taste. To assemble the
cake, remove the greaseproof paper from both sponges.
Drizzle each one with a little sherry if you like. Spread

the cream over one of the sponges, then sprinkle the fruit on top. Sandwich the second sponge on top and press down. Run a knife around the edge of the cake to smooth it off and drizzle over your chocolate topping. Happy days, you've done it! But allow the chocolate topping to firm up slightly before tucking in.

Rice pudding

Sometimes the golden oldies are the best! This rice pudding is dead easy, very comforting and can be varied with all types of different flavours.

Serves 4
100g/3½oz butter • 115g/4oz caster sugar •
1.3 litres/2 pints milk • seeds from 2 vanilla pods •
a pinch of salt • 140g/5oz pudding rice

Put the butter, sugar, milk, vanilla seeds, salt and rice in a pan and bring to a gentle simmer. Cover and leave to simmer until the milk has been absorbed and the rice is soft but not too stodgy. Serve in bowls while hot.

Try this: For a nice surprise, drop a spoonful of jam into the middle of each pudding, or melt about 200g of best-quality cooking chocolate (70% cocoa solids) in a bowl over some simmering water and stir this into your rice pudding before serving.

Baileys and banana bread and butter pudding

Having grown up in a pub, two of the alcoholic drinks I tried and got a taste for at a very early age were Baileys and a cocktail called a Snowball. However, now I'm older I detest the taste of both of them! Jools has a little drop of Baileys every now and again, so there's usually a bottle hanging about, and one day I had some bananas and it was as simple as that – I tried this recipe out and it was fantastic, one of the best possible twists on a bread and butter pudding.

Serves about 6

½ a loaf of pre-sliced white bread, crusts removed •
55g/2oz or ¼ pack of butter, softened • 140g/5oz
caster sugar • seeds from 1 vanilla pod • 8 free-range
eggs • 500ml/18fl oz double cream • 565ml/1 pint
milk • 4 shots of Baileys • 5 bananas •
4 tablespoons flaked almonds, toasted until golden •
icing sugar to dust

Preheat the oven to 180°C/350°F/gas 4. Press each slice of bread down to get them as flat as possible. Butter each piece thinly but thoroughly with the softened butter, then cut the slices of bread in half and put to one side.

In a bowl whisk together the sugar, vanilla seeds and eggs till pale and fluffy, then add the cream, the milk and the Baileys and whisk until smooth. Slice up your peeled bananas and lightly toast your almonds in the preheated oven. Take an appropriately sized baking dish (or you could do individual ones) and rub the sides with a little butter. Dip each piece of bread in the egg mixture then begin to layer the bread, the sliced banana and the almonds in the baking dish. Repeat until everything has been used up, ending with a top layer of bread. Pour over the rest of your egg mixture, using your fingers to pat down the bread to make sure it soaks up all the lovely flavours.

Generously dust the top of the pudding with icing sugar and bake in the oven for around 35 minutes or until the custard has set around the outside but is slightly wobbly in the centre. Allow it to cool and firm up slightly. Some people like to serve it with ice cream or double cream, but if you get it gooey enough in the middle then it is nice just on its own. Feel free to take this recipe in any direction you like – using raisins or dried apricots or different types of bread like brioche or pannetone.

PENGUIN SPECIAL
The Life and Times of Allen Lane
Jeremy Lewis

Penguin Special is the story of how a stocky, 'unbookish' Bristolian went on to found the most famous publishing house in the world. As well as providing a comprehensive account of Allen Lane's achievements both as the founder and head of a company that had a major influence on the life of post-war Britain, Jeremy Lewis's highly entertaining biography also reveals a mischievous, often contradictory and oddly endearing figure who loathed meetings and paperwork, insisted on the best writers and academics despite his own lack of formal education, and struggled to come to terms with the 1960s Britain that Penguin itself had helped to usher in. Published on the occasion of Penguin's 70th birthday, *Penguin Special* is a superlative portrait of the greatest publisher of the twentieth century.

May 2005 ISBN 0670914851 £25

PENGUIN BY DESIGN
A Cover Story 1935–2005
Phil Baines

Published to coincide with Penguin's 70th birthday and a major display at the V&A, *Penguin by Design* is a celebration of the rich and diverse design heritage of Penguin book covers. Beautifully illustrated throughout and written by a leading design writer, *Penguin by Design* is required reading for anybody interested not only in the evolution of the Penguin brand but also in the development of British publishing and graphic design as a profession.

May 2005 ISBN 0713998393 £15

To order a copy of either of these books, simply call Penguin Books c/o Bookpost on **01624 677237** and have your credit/debit card ready. Alternatively e-mail your order to bookshop@enterprise.net Postage and package is free in mainland UK. Overseas customers must add £2 per book. Price and availability subject to change without notice.